COLONIAL PEOPLE

The Barber

ANN HEINRICHS

Marshall Cavendish
Benchmark
New York

Website: www.marshallcavendish.us

This publication represents the opinions and views of the author based on Ann Heinrich's personal experience, knowledge, and research. The information in this book serves as a general guide only. The author and publisher have used their best efforts in preparing this book and disclaim liability rising directly and indirectly from the use and application of this book.

Other Marshall Cavendish Offices:

Marshall Cavendish International (Asia) Private Limited, 1 New Industrial Road, Singapore 536196 • Marshall Cavendish International (Thailand) Co Ltd. 253 Asoke, 12th Flr, Sukhumvit 21 Road, Klongtoey Nua, Wattana, Bangkok 10110, Thailand • Marshall Cavendish (Malaysia) Sdn Bhd, Times Subang, Lot 46, Subang Hi-Tech Industrial Park, Batu Tiga, 40000 Shah Alam, Selangor Darul Ehsan, Malaysia

Marshall Cavendish is a trademark of Times Publishing Limited

All websites were available and accurate when this book was sent to press.

Library of Congress Cataloging-in-Publication Data

Heinrichs, Ann.
The barber / by Ann Heinrichs. — 1st ed.
p. cm. — (Colonial people)
Includes bibliographical references and index.
Summary: "Explore the life of a colonial barber and his importance to the community, as well as everyday life, responsibilities, and social practices during that time"—Provided by publisher.
ISBN 978-0-7614-4800-6
1. Barbers—United States—History—17th century—Juvenile literature. 2. United States—History—Colonial period, ca. 1600–1775—Juvenile literature. I. Title.
TT956.H36 2010
646.7'240973—dc22
2009018626

Editor: Christine Florie
Publisher: Michelle Bisson
Art Director: Anahid Hamparian
Series Designer: Kay Petronio

Expert Readers: Paul Douglas Newman, Ph.D., Department of History, University of Pittsburgh at Johnstown; staff member, The Wig Shop at Colonial Williamsburg, Williamsburg, VA

Photo research by Marybeth Kavanagh

Cover photo by Yale Center for British Art, Paul Mellon Collection, USA/The Bridgeman Art Library

The photographs in this book are used by permission and through the courtesy of:
The Colonial Williamsburg Foundation: 4, 20, 26, 29, 31; Abby Aldrich Rockefeller Folk Art Museum, Gift of Ellin and Baron Gordon, 7; *Art Resource, NY*: HIP, 9; *The Art Archive*: São Paulo Art Museum Brazil/Gianni Dagli Orti, 11; *The Granger Collection*: 12, 34; *Getty Images*: Hulton Archive, 16, 22, 39; Stock Montage, 37; *North Wind Picture Archives*: 17; *The Image Works* Mary Evans Picture Library, 40

Printed in Malaysia (T)
1 3 5 6 4 2

CONTENTS

ONE

The Barber's Changing Role

Barber, barber, shave a pig.

How many hairs to make a wig?

Four and twenty, that's enough.

Give the barber a pinch of snuff.

Children in England used to sing this nursery rhyme. Another favorite rhyme tells about Old Mother Hubbard and her dog:

She went to the barber's

To buy him a wig;

But when she came back

He was dancing a jig.

The colonial barber was a skilled craftsman, and many depended on his trade.

These verses give us some clues about what English barbers used to do. They shaved people, and they made wigs. As we shall see, they did much more than that, too.

Barbers were skilled craftspeople in a well-respected trade. They offered valuable services to their European customers. Barbers were just as useful to the American **colonists**. The colonists had left their homelands to start a new life. Some hoped to make money in a land rich with natural resources. Some wanted to practice their religion freely. Many simply wanted to make a fresh start. One and all, they made the long sea voyage across the Atlantic Ocean.

The colonists established thirteen colonies along the Atlantic coast. These colonies were ruled by England from about 1607 until 1783. This is known as the **colonial** period. By 1770 more than 2 million people lived in the American colonies. Among them were people skilled in many trades. There were blacksmiths, shipbuilders, carpenters, tailors, shoemakers, printers, bakers, barbers, and many others. Some cities even had a number of barber shops, each employing several barbers.

The Barber-Surgeons

Barbers have been cutting hair and shaving beards for thousands of years. In fact, the word "barber" comes from *barba*, the ancient

Latin word for "beard." Eventually, barbers' duties expanded. By the 1100s they were performing minor surgery, such as treating wounds and pulling teeth. They also practiced bleeding, or cutting a patient's arm to let some blood out. "Bad blood" or too much blood was once believed to cause many illnesses. In this new role, barbers were called barber-surgeons.

The Barber Pole

Barber-surgeons advertised their shops by hanging a barber pole outside the door. The pole had red and white swirling stripes, like a candy cane. The red color represented blood, and the white stood for bandages. Long after barbers stopped practicing surgery, barber poles used red, white, and blue stripes (right). Some historians say the blue color represents veins. Others say the blue originates from an English law in the 1700s. It required barbers to display a blue-and-white pole, while surgeons were to use the same colored pole with a red rag attached. Some say American barbers used the three-color pole to match the colors of the U.S. flag.

In 1540 barber-surgeons in England formed the Company of Barber-Surgeons. This was a craft **guild**, or organization of tradespeople. Officers of the guild inspected its members to make sure they did their jobs properly. Barber-surgeons practiced their trade in the colonies, too. In 1630, three barber-surgeons from England landed in Boston, Massachusetts. One of them, William Dinly, later died in a snowstorm on his way to pull a tooth.

Over time, surgery came to play a smaller role in the barber-surgeon's practice. In 1745 an English law made barber and surgeon two separate professions. Barbers in the colonies gradually abandoned surgery, too, leaving that role to **apothecaries**. Barbers had plenty of other work to do, though. By then they had taken on a new craft: wig making.

Enter the Wig

Men's wigs first became fashionable in France. King Louis XIII of France was embarrassed that his hair was thinning. To cover his head, he began wearing a wig in 1624. His son, King Louis XIV, kept up the trend. His wigs were huge masses of curls that flowed down below his shoulders. The fashion soon spread to England, where King Charles II sported his own fancy wigs. The noblemen in his court, quick to imitate their king, wore wigs, too. Soon no fine gentleman in England would appear in public without his wig.

The name for wigs also came from France. In French a wig is a *perruque* (pronounced peh-ROOK). People in England spelled that word "peruke." Eventually, the word changed to "periwig," which was shortened to "wig."

The wig craze quickly spread from England to the American colonies. For barbers the new popularity of wigs was great for business. Wigs were expensive creations. Making a wig brought in much more money than shaving, pulling teeth, or bleeding a customer. Wigs were no longer just a way to cover up bald heads. For a well-dressed, respectable man, they were an essential part of his wardrobe.

King Charles II of England wore wigs like those styled in France. Soon, this fashion trend spread to the colonies in America.

Hairstyles in the Colonies

The earliest American colonists wore their own natural hair. Men who worked on farms or hunted in the woods had no use for wigs or fancy hairstyles. At most, they tied their hair back in a ponytail or a braided pigtail.

Members of certain religious groups did not wear wigs, either. Groups such as the **Quakers** and the **Puritans** believed wigs were a sign of boastful pride. Before they left England, the Puritans were called Roundheads. That was because they wore their hair short. They opposed King Charles and the long-haired wigs fashionable in his court. The Puritans went on to establish the Massachusetts Bay Colony and other settlements.

In their Sunday sermons ministers preached against the foolish practice of wearing wigs. Many young men ignored the warnings, though. In time, few could resist the temptation to follow the current fashions. Eventually, even ministers began wearing wigs.

Big Hair for the Bigwigs

At first, wig wearers were the leading citizens in colonial cities and towns. They were government officials, wealthy merchants, lawyers, and prosperous landowners. Because of this fact, the term "bigwig" came to mean an important person. In upper-class

Children of wealthy colonial American families wore wigs.

families even children wore wigs. A boy might get his first wig at the age of seven.

In the southern colonies wealthy plantation owners wore wigs. They provided wigs for some of their African-American slaves as well. Plantation owners often insisted on white or light gray wigs for their male servants who worked in public settings, such as butlers, servers, doormen, and coachmen.

In time the style trickled down to all levels of society.

Most Colonial women styled their own hair instead of wearing wigs. This is Martha Jefferson Randolph, daughter of President Thomas Jefferson.

Ordinary tradespeople, such as blacksmiths and innkeepers, used the wig maker's services. Even poor people could be seen wearing cheap, poor-quality wigs. For many, wearing a wig was as normal as wearing a suit is today.

In France both men and women wore wigs. French ladies' wigs were awesome. They could be as tall as 3 feet. Some wigs even had strings of pearls, artificial birds, and model ships woven in with the hair! In the colonies, women rarely wore wigs. Instead, they adorned their own hair with curls, braids, or extensions they purchased. Some barbers sold women's curls, and a few styled women's hair. However, most colonial barbers offered services only to men. Barbering and wig making were sometimes separate trades. Not all barbers made wigs, but most wig makers were also barbers.

TWO

A Day in the Barber's Shop

A gentleman strolls down the wooden walkway in his coat, waistcoat, knee breeches, white stockings, and buckled shoes. Cows graze on the village green, and boys run by, rolling hoops down the street. The milkman rumbles along, his cart filled with copper milk cans. From the second floor of the inn, a maid tosses a pail of dirty water into the street. The gentleman dodges it just in time.

Continuing on, he passes the baker, the hatter, the blacksmith, and the shoemaker. He knows the shops by their signs. Some are wooden planks painted with names such as King George's Tavern. They are decorated with colorful pictures—a lion, an eagle, a rooster, or a whale. Some signs are a large object, such as a horseshoe, a wagon wheel, or a hat. At last the gentleman arrives at the sign reading "Barber and Peruke Maker."

Making a Colonial Shop Sign

Merchants and craftspeople in colonial times hung colorful signs in front of their shops. Often a sign displayed a picture as a symbol of a trade. As people walked along, they could see the picture even before they were close enough to read the words.

Things You Will Need

A sheet of paper
A large sheet of white cardboard
A pencil
Colored markers, crayons, or washable paints

Directions

Choose one of these trades:

TRADE	SYMBOL
Barber	a wig
Baker	a loaf of bread
Blacksmith	a horseshoe
Cooper	a barrel
Hatter	a hat
Shoemaker	a shoe or boot
Wheelwright	a wagon wheel

Read all the directions, and sketch out your sign design on a piece of paper. Then transfer the design onto the cardboard.

1. To begin your design on paper, make a decorative border around the edges of the sign.

2. Print your last name at the top of the sign and your trade at the bottom.

3. Draw the symbol in a large size in the center.

4. Copy this design onto the cardboard in pencil.

5. Now add colors over your pencil drawing. Use bold colors that can be seen from far away. Red, blue, gold (or yellow), and black were often used.

6. Add more decorations if you like, such as stars or banners.

7. Hang your colonial sign on your door, refrigerator, or bulletin board. Can you give some details about what you do in your trade?

The Shop

As the gentleman enters, he smells the sharp aroma of perfume and scented oils. Tiny grains of powder floating in the air tickle his nose. Around the shop he sees a half-dozen men and boys at work. They are busy shaving faces and heads, combing out hair, or laboring over wig stands. One man is the master barber, who owns the shop. The others are **apprentices** and **journeymen**.

The colonial barbershop was a busy place where workers gave male customers shaves, as well as made and powdered wigs.

At the time, serving an apprenticeship was the only way a boy could learn a trade. (Girls could be apprentices, too, but most were boys.) An apprentice worked for his master for seven years. In return the master taught him every aspect of the trade. The master also provided the apprentice with food, clothing, and a home. After seven years the apprentice became a journeyman. Then he could work for any master and receive wages for his work. Some journeymen saved money in the hope of opening their own shops someday.

The master barber greets the customer and asks how he can be of service. Today, the gentleman needs his regular Saturday shave. Beards and mustaches were not fashionable in colonial times. It was said that only **frontiersmen** and pirates wore beards. Townspeople looked down on unshaven men and even made fun of them. Some men shaved themselves at home. But many others stopped into the barber shop for a shave once or twice a week. Those who could afford it even had a shave every day.

The Shave

The gentleman settles back into the barber's chair. As he gazes around the shop, he sees shelves filled with colored bottles and jars. They hold all sorts of creams, oils, lotions, and perfumes. Wigs in various styles are mounted on the walls or displayed in the window. An apprentice tucks a barber's apron underneath the gentleman's chin to keep his clothes clean. Then the barber

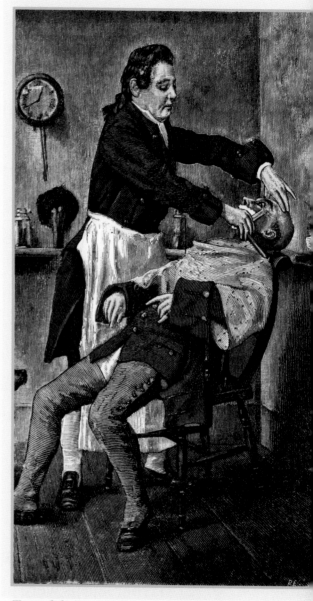

Facial hair, such as beards and mustaches, was not popular during colonial times. Many men visited the barber for their shave.

takes down a shaving bowl from its hook on the wall. It is a shallow bowl with a half-circle cut out of its wide, flat brim. The cutout fits right up against the customer's neck.

The barber fills the bowl with hot water and drops a soap ball in. Then he takes a shaving brush made from the stiff hairs of a badger. He swirls it in the bowl to make suds and soaps up the customer's face. The warm soap makes the customer's skin soft and slippery, preventing nicks and cuts. The barber unfolds a sharp steel razor from its leather covering. Carefully, with downward strokes, he shaves the gentleman's face.

Finally, he splashes the customer's face with perfume or a scented **tonic**. Bay rum was a popular aftershave tonic. It was made of rum mixed with crushed bay leaves. This liquid gave off a sharp, spicy aroma and masked body odors. In colonial times people did not take baths every day. It was more common to bathe once every month or two. Now clean-shaven and fragrant, the customer is on his way.

All the News of the Day

Barber shops were popular places to get news and hear daily gossip. A good barber kept a supply of newspapers in his shop. Customers could read them while they waited for their turn in the barber's chair. The newspapers gave them plenty to talk about. Typical news stories told about lost or stolen horses, land or houses for sale, or a runaway servant or wife. Perhaps a new schoolteacher arrived in town or a prisoner escaped from jail. One newspaper told of a recent shipwreck. Another reported an "abundance of dead fish" floating near the shore.

News of discontent in the colonies was an especially interesting topic. England was making the colonists pay taxes on more and more items. The colonists could do nothing about it. They had no representatives who could vote in England's parliament, or lawmaking body. Many colonists began to demand "No taxation without representation!" Conflicts with the British would eventually lead to the Revolutionary War (1775–1783). This war would free the colonists from English rule.

Dressing a Wig

Another customer arrives carrying a wig box. Inside is his wig, and he wants it dressed. Dressing a wig means fixing it up and restyling it. Wigs required constant care. They had to be cleaned, trimmed, curled, and sometimes powdered regularly. The barber promises to have his apprentice deliver the wig the next day.

He looks over his collection of wig blocks to find the right

A barber begins work on a wig after it has been attached to a wig block at a re-created barbershop in Colonial Williamsburg, Virginia.

size. Wig blocks were head-shaped blocks of wood designed for holding wigs. In fact, the word "blockhead" comes from the early days of wig blocks. People used the word to refer to a stupid person. The barber tacks the wig to the block and starts to work.

Some barbers curl hair with metal curling irons heated in an oven. Others use clay curlers about 3 inches long. In that case the barber wraps each lock of hair around a curler and fastens it in place. Then he bakes the wig in an oven to set the curls. After a good baking, he removes the curlers. To hold the hair in place, he smears it with a generous amount of **pomatum**. This oily grease was made from animal fat. Taking his comb and scissors, he reshapes the curls and trims any stray ends.

Finally, the barber carries the wig to the powder room to apply the powder. Wigs could be powdered with brown, black, or gray powder to help maintain their natural color. By the mid–1700s, however, styles were changing, and white wigs were fashionable for formal occasions. To make wigs white, barbers powdered them with flour, starch, white clay, or plaster dust. Some customers asked for blue, purple, pink, or yellow wigs, so that called for colored powder. Wig powder was often scented with flowers or fragrant herbs, such as lavender.

The Powder Room

Many colonial barbers had a little room in their shop called the powder room. It was not much bigger than a closet. That was where they put powder on their wigs. The powder-room door had a top half and a bottom half. Opening the top half, the barber held the wig inside the room. He dusted a generous amount of powder onto the wig with a powder puff or sprayed the powder through a tube. The bottom half of the door kept the powder from drifting all over the shop. Some upper-class homes also had powder rooms.

Large ballrooms had powder rooms, too. Men would visit the powder room during a festive evening so a barber could repowder their wigs. As the barber applied the powder, the man wore a mask to keep it off his face and out of his nose.

Paying the Barber

Many customers paid the barber annually. Once a year they paid for a year's worth of shaving, wig dressing, and new wigs. Some customers paid in coins or paper money. Many different types of money were circulating in the colonies then. Most colonists used Spanish dollars or English pounds, shillings, and pence.

So Many Ways to Pay

Colonial leaders knew that money was scarce. Some colonies passed laws declaring that certain goods could be used to pay debts or taxes. In the Virginia colony people could pay for things with tobacco, wool, or lumber. They could also use flax, a fiber used for making linen cloth, or hemp, a fiber for making ropes. In Pennsylvania and Maryland colonists could pay their debts in flax and hemp. Wool became a standard form of payment in the Rhode Island colony. In Massachusetts and New Hampshire people could pay their taxes with flax, hemp, leather, or oil. They could also pay with tar or turpentine, which were used in shipbuilding.

Money, however, was in short supply. Quite a few customers paid in **barter**, or trade. One customer, for example, paid his barber by giving him some horses. In the Virginia colony tobacco was the major crop. Many Virginia customers paid their barbers with tobacco or notes of tobacco ownership. Still, every barber had a few customers who never paid their bills. Either they were short of money or they just forgot to pay. Barbers were constantly bringing customers to court to demand payment of their bills.

Late afternoon was delivery time. That was when the barber sent his apprentices out to deliver freshly dressed wigs. The busiest time of all was Saturday afternoon. Every fine gentleman needed his wig to wear at the evening's events. Apprentices welcomed this chance to get out of the shop and enjoy the fresh air. Off they ran with their wig boxes in hand, scurrying through the narrow lanes.

THREE

Making a Wig

On this day a customer enters the shop asking for a brand-new wig. Wigs were the most expensive items the barber sold. A new wig could cost as much as a man's entire wardrobe of hat, coat, shirt, breeches, stockings, and shoes. Wigs were uncomfortable, too. They were itchy, heavy, and hot. They were hard to keep on straight. The powder flaked off onto their clothes and blew off in a stiff wind. Nevertheless, a wig was the mark of a fine gentleman.

First, the customer has to choose a style. Gentlemen in France wore an amazing variety of wigs. The French *Encyclopédie Perruquière*, or *Encyclopedia of Wigs*, published in 1762, showed dozens of different styles. Some featured corkscrew curls and multiple pigtails. There were high-rise creations with bushy curls flowing down to the waist. The American colonists, however, wore less flamboyant styles.

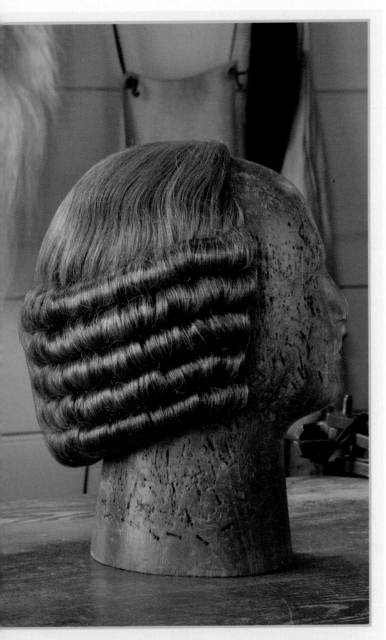

Bob wigs were the most popular style worn in the colonies.

A Style for Every Taste

One of the most popular wigs for everyday use was the bob wig. It was a short wig with rows of curls that fit closely around the sides and back of the head. The club wig was a simpler style with fewer curls.

The tie wig was popular, too. It featured a ponytail tied at the back of the neck with a black ribbon. The queue wig was similar. Instead of a ponytail, it had a queue, or braided pigtail, in the back.

Campaign wigs were first introduced for soldiers. Soon others wore them, too. They featured short side curls and a short queue. One type of campaign wig was the Ramillies wig. It had puffier side curls and a long queue. A big bow was tied at the top of the queue, and a smaller bow adorned the bottom.

The bag wig was another fashionable style. It had long hair in the back that was tied up in a black silk or satin bag. Full-bottomed wigs were long and tightly curled. They reached almost down to the waist. Growing dizzy from considering all his choices, the customer settles on a simple bob wig.

Wig Materials and Colors

Barbers made wigs out of all kinds of materials, including goat hair and horse manes. Some wigs were made from the hair of yaks. These shaggy, long-haired animals live high in the Himalaya Mountains of Asia. But the finest, most expensive wigs were made of human hair.

Most colonial barbers imported their wig hair from England. One Virginia barber placed a newspaper ad saying, "Just arrived, a choice Parcel of Hairs, prepared by the best Hands in London." Another advertised "A Fresh Cargoe of live human Hairs, already curl'd and well prepared." A New York wig maker declared, "Morrison, peruke maker from London, . . . has a choice parcel of human, horse and goat's hair to dispose of."

Wigs came in a variety of colors. Some of the most popular shades were black, white, brown, and flaxen, or blond. Another favorite color was grizzle, a mixture of black and white hair.

Today, we call this color combination "salt and pepper." Off-white, yellowish, chestnut, and gray were less popular shades.

In the early 1700s wigs in lighter shades began to come into fashion. Barbers could not always get hold of light-colored wig hair. At first they tried to bleach the hair to lighten it up, but the results were not very good. Then they began to dust their wigs with white powder.

Public Times

In the Virginia colony the barber's busiest times were the Public Times. These festive days took place twice a year, when Virginia's court and lawmaking assembly met in Williamsburg, the colonial capital. Hundreds of other citizens came, too, for this was the height of the social season. There were receptions, balls, theater performances, horse races, and many other forms of entertainment. These events gave people an opportunity to show off their finest clothes. As Public Times approached, the barber worked long hours. All his customers needed freshly dressed wigs or brand-new ones so they could look their best.

Preparing the Customer's Head

The first order of business is to shave the customer's head. A wig could only be fitted to a clean-shaven **scalp**. A journeyman takes care of this shaving job. Once the customer's head is clean and shiny, it can be measured.

The master barber takes a long strip of paper, about 1 inch wide. He will take measurements along this strip. First, he measures from the top of the forehead, over the head, to the **nape** of the neck. Then he snips a notch into the paper strip and labels it. Four more measurements are needed. He measures the back of the head from **temple** to temple, the back from cheek to cheek, the top of the head from ear to ear, and the upper curve of the forehead.

It will take a week or more to build the wig. So the customer must go home

A customer tries on his new wig in this re-created barbershop in Colonial Williamsburg, Virginia.

with a shaved head. To cover it up, he puts on a silk or velvet cap or a turban. After he gets his wig, he will wear this head covering whenever he takes his wig off at night.

Building the Wig

The barber chooses the wig hair, and his apprentices and journeymen prepare it. First, they sprinkle the hair with sand or flour, which draws out any grease or oil, and shake it off. Next, they comb the hair through a sort of metal-toothed brush called a hackle. Then they separate the hair into small sections. To make the hair curly, they roll each section of hair round and round on a clay curler. Then they put the curlers into a pot of water and boil them for three hours. After boiling, the curlers are put into a small oven to bake. This makes sure the hair will stay curly. Metal curling irons were sometimes used instead, without the boiling and baking.

Meanwhile, the barber makes a wig pattern on paper. It shows how many rows of hair the wig will need, the length of each row, and the length of hair for each location. Then he uses his notched measuring strip to make a **caul** out of net fabric and strips of ribbon. It is exactly the size and shape of the customer's head. He tacks the caul to a wig block.

When the curlers come out of the oven, the barber's workers

A barber separates hair that will be used to build a wig at a re-created barbershop in Colonial Williamsburg, Virginia.

unroll the hair. Following the barber's pattern, they weave the root ends of the hairs into lengths of silk thread. This creates long strips of hair, with the curly parts hanging down like tassels or fringe. Then, strip by strip, the barber sews the hair onto the caul, starting at the nape of the neck. He sews each strip about one-fourth of an inch from the one before.

Now the wig is almost done. To set the style, the barber applies pomatum until the wig is practically hard. Then he might attach a drawstring so the customer can tie it firmly on his head. The finished product is a work of art. The apprentice can deliver it the next day. Pleased with his masterpiece, the barber washes his hands, dismisses his helpers, closes the shop, and goes home.

FOUR

The Barber's Community

Like other colonists, the barber depended on many tradespeople in the community. The tailor made his clothes, and the shoemaker crafted his shoes. The hatter made his cocked hat, the three-cornered hat popular in colonial times. The chandler made candles so the barber and his family could see at night. When they were sick, they got medicine from the apothecary.

The barber needed local tradespeople to help him run his business, too. For example, the washerwoman cleaned his towels and aprons. A traveling scissors-grinder sharpened his scissors. Hair and powder came from the miller's flour mill. The printer published the barber's ads in his newspaper and printed **handbills** to post in public. Woodworkers and bakers were helpful, too.

The Woodworkers

Woodworkers made many items the barber used. The blocker, also called the blockhead carver or block cutter, carved wooden wig blocks. Every barber who made wigs needed several of these head-shaped stands for building wigs, dressing them, and displaying them in the window. Some wig blocks were even built with a little door on the side that opened on hinges. The chamber inside was a good place for storing wig-making tools, combs, or pins.

The joiner was another useful woodworker. He made boxes, chests, drawers, and other items that had corners. Without using nails, he joined pieces of wood with dovetail joints, which fit together like interlocking fingers. Barbers relied on joiners for their wig boxes. These were square wooden boxes with a handle on top. Inside was a wooden post where the wig sat. People took wigs to and from the barber shop in wig boxes, and wig owners could carry them when they traveled.

Turners were woodworkers who cut decorative patterns around columns of wood. They made furniture legs, bedposts, and balusters, the posts alongside staircases. For barbers the turner made wig stands. These were chest-high wooden posts with a rounded bulb on the top. People also used wig stands at home when they took their wigs off at night. Eventually, tradespeople called cabinetmakers performed many of these woodworking tasks in one shop.

Colonial bakers were very helpful to barbers. They would bake hair curlers in bread dough, creating locks of tightly curled hair for wigs.

The Baker

The barber and the baker had a close working relationship. Their connection is a surprising one. When making a wig, the barber bakes the curled-up locks of hair in an oven so they stay curly. However, his little oven does not always do the trick. In that case, the barber piles the curlers, still wound with hair, onto a tray. Then he has his apprentice take it to the baker's shop.

The baker knows what to do. He has done this many times before. He rolls out two round sheets of bread dough. He seals the mound of curlers inside the dough, just as if they were the filling for a pie. Then he puts this "loaf" in the oven and bakes it. When the barber gets it back, he breaks open the bread crust and removes the steamy curlers. When he unwinds the hair, it is now quite firmly curled!

Making a Good Impression

Colonial barbers played an important role in the community. The colonists were building a new nation from the ground up. They were growing new businesses, a new government, new ways of life, and new ideas about freedom. They had to prove to themselves, and to the world, that they could work together as a nation.

Some colonial officials were Englishmen appointed by the king. Others were colonists who had risen to leadership positions. Colonial leaders were in the public eye. They often met with important people from England, France, and other countries. They knew the value of clothing and hair fashions. If they presented a fine appearance, others would take them seriously. They believed that if they *looked* superior, they *were* superior. Thus, the barber helped colonial leaders uphold their status in the community.

Colonial Leaders and Their Wigs

Edward Charlton was one of the leading barbers and wig makers in Williamsburg, Virginia. This city was the Virginia colony's capital from 1699 to 1780. Many great colonial leaders lived and worked

The Wig Tax

In 1730 the New York colony passed a wig tax. The tax money was used to support English soldiers stationed in New York. It called for ". . . a tax of three shillings Current mony of this Colony to be paid by every Inhabitant Resident or **Sojourner** of and in this Colony young and old . . . as shall wear a whigg or Peruke made of Human or horse hair or mixt."

Notice that many words in this law have unusual spellings. That is because in colonial times, standard spellings for English words had not yet been established.

in Williamsburg. They all needed wigs to look their best. Several of these men were regular customers in Edward Charlton's shop.

One was Thomas Jefferson. He was the main author of the Declaration of Independence, which the colonists issued on July 4, 1776. Later, Jefferson became the third U.S. president. Charlton's account books show that Jefferson bought four wigs from his shop. He got a queue wig, a tie wig, and two bob wigs. This notable gentleman also purchased two pairs of curls and 3 pounds of hair powder.

Another customer of Charlton's was Patrick Henry. Henry was famous for his fiery speech declaring, "Give me liberty, or give me death!" This speech convinced Virginians to join the Revolutionary War. Patrick Henry bought only one wig from Charlton, and he never went back to have it dressed. Henry must have visited other barbers, though. A friend recalled that he "always appeared in . . . a tye wig, which was dressed and powdered in the highest style."

One famous colonist did not wear wigs. It was George Washington, who became the first U.S. president. Washington wore his own natural hair. However, he did curl it and powder it white. George Washington led the colonial army in the Revolutionary War. That war would mark a turning point in the colonial barber's role.

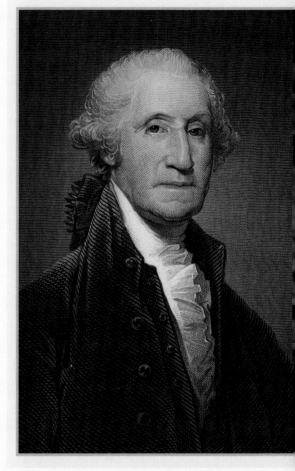

President George Washington was not fond of wigs. He chose to wear his own hair curled and powdered.

FIVE

New Hairstyles for a New Nation

By the late 1770s colonial barbers were losing much of their wig business. People were developing new attitudes and values. In the Declaration of Independence the colonists had declared that all people are equal. They rejected the idea of kings and noblemen. With the Revolutionary War they gained freedom from England and its king. The thirteen colonies then became the first thirteen states of the new United States. This was a victory for common people and social equality. Some people continued to wear wigs, but wigs were no longer the status symbol they once were. Others, rejecting the upper-class fashions of the past, stopped wearing wigs altogether.

A New Scene at the Barber Shop

In the new United States younger men led the way in introducing new hairstyles. Instead of wearing wigs, they wore their natural hair.

Benjamin Franklin and His Wig

Benjamin Franklin was a colonial newspaper publisher, inventor, and **diplomat**. During the Revolutionary War the colonial government sent him to France. He was to urge King Louis XVI to support the colonists in the war against England.

Franklin did not like wearing wigs. The top of his head was bald, and wigs made his scalp itch. On a 1776 visit to Paris, France, Franklin wore a fur hat (below). The French people fell in love with his natural, down-to-earth style. They treated him almost like a rock star. Medals, plates, and jewelry were imprinted with Franklin's image, complete with fur hat.

On a 1778 visit, Franklin was to meet with the king himself. For this grand occasion he ordered a wig. After all, everyone at the French court would be wearing one—including the king.

When the wig maker brought Franklin his wig, he tried it on and cast it aside with disgust. It was too small, he said. "No, monsieur!" cried the wig maker. "It is not the wig which is too small; it is your head which is too large!" Franklin appeared bare-headed before the king, who welcomed him graciously. Once he was back home, Franklin chose to wear his wigs only on special occasions.

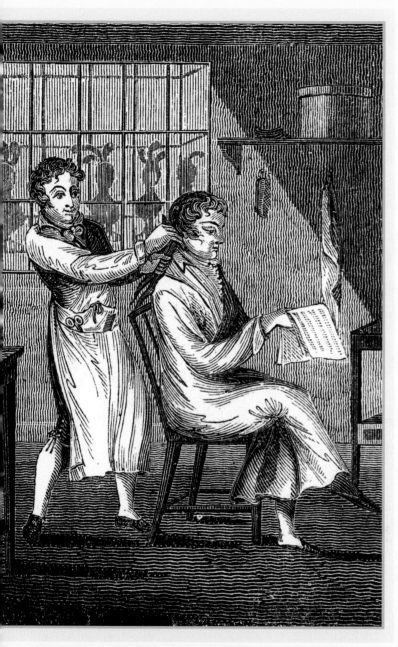

As styles changed, men no longer wore wigs. Instead, they spent hours in the barbershop having their own hair cut and styled.

Even so, men still visited the barber, especially the older men. They still wanted their hair to be curled and lightly powdered.

Although wigs were out of style, many men still preferred "big hair." Some wore mounds of curls all over their heads. Others grew their hair long in back so they could have a queue and tie it with a bow. Their visits to the barber shop took longer than they had in the days of wigs. These sessions were probably more painful, too.

Customers now sat in the barber's chair for up to an hour or more. Using heated curlers, the barber rolled up locks of their hair. Former wig customers were not used to this. The hot curlers probably burned their scalps.

After the curlers were out, the barber trimmed, combed, and styled the hair. All this pulling and yanking was probably uncomfortable, too. At last, the barber applied some powder. Now he used hair powder in natural shades instead of white.

A Declining Trade

The barber still had a few wig customers. Older men still wore white-powdered wigs. They remembered their younger days, when a white wig was the sign of a fine gentleman. However, the wig-making part of the business would never be the same as it was in the golden era of wigs. This period had lasted more than 150 years. Some barbers adapted their skills to the changing hair fashions. However, many who had thrived as wig makers in colonial times went out of business. Some pursued other types of work, but others never recovered.

For the sad tale of one barber's fate, consider George Lafong. He had been a prosperous barber and wig maker in Williamsburg, Virginia. One of his customers was George Washington. Lafong dressed Washington's hair and also sold curls to Washington's stepdaughter, Patsy Custis. In 1773 Lafong advertised that he had hired a barber from London, England. This man could style hair in the newest, most elegant fashions. He could also provide ladies with "headdresses so natural as not to be distinguished by the most curious Eye."

It seemed that Lafong's business was doing well. However, in 1776, he placed a newspaper ad demanding payment from those who owed him money. He said that he was having trouble supporting his family and that he himself was in debt. Lafong's money troubles must have continued. In 1796 he was seen on the streets of Norfolk, Virginia. He was a beggar.

Barbers did not disappear from the American scene. Hair would always need to be trimmed and styled. Wig making would even continue to be a fine craft into the twenty-first century. Yet the glorious days of the colonial barber's trade had come to an end.

Glossary

apothecaries	druggists who mix ingredients to make medicines
apprentices	young people who train under a master craftsperson to learn a trade
barter	trading one item or service for another
caul	the net cap on which a wig is built
colonial	relating to colonies
colonists	people who settle a new land for their home country
diplomat	a person sent from one country to another as a government representative
frontiersmen	rough, hardy people who work in wild, unsettled places
guild	an association of people working in a certain trade
handbills	sheets of paper advertising an event, product, or service
journeymen	tradespeople who have completed an apprenticeship
nape	the part of the neck where the hairline ends
pomatum	an oily substance for dressing hair; also called pomade
Puritans	members of a religious group that opposed overly ornamented churches and religious items and luxurious personal attire
Quakers	members of a religious group that began as a movement to return to the early Christians' simple way of life; later renamed the Religious Society of Friends
scalp	the skin on the head
sojourner	a temporary resident
temple	the spot on the side of the head at eye level
tonic	a liquid that refreshes or stimulates the skin

Find Out More

BOOKS

Calkhoven, Laurie. *George Washington: An American Life.* New York: Sterling, 2007.

Giblin, James Cross, and Michael Dooling (illustrator). *The Amazing Life of Benjamin Franklin.* New York: Scholastic Paperbacks, 2006.

Kalman, Bobby. *A Visual Dictionary of a Colonial Community.* New York: Crabtree Publishing, 2008.

Petersen, Christine. *The Apothecary.* New York: Marshall Cavendish, 2010.

Roberts, Russell. *Life in Colonial America.* Hockessin, DE: Mitchell Lane Publishers, 2007.

Sheinkin, Steve. *The American Revolution.* Stamford, CT: Summer Street Press, 2005.

Winters, Kay, and Larry Day (illustrator). *Colonial Voices: Hear Them Speak.* New York: Dutton Children's Books, 2008.

WEBSITES

Colonial Kids: A Celebration of Life in the 1700s

library.thinkquest.org/J002611F/

Find out what colonial children wore, what their communities were like, and how they worked and played.

Colonial Williamsburg Trades

www.colonialwilliamsburg.org/Almanack/life/trades/tradehdr.cfm

This site explains many colonial trades, including those of the barber and wig maker.

Liberty's Kids: Now and Then

www.libertyskids.com/nowthen/index.html

Here you will learn about life in the 1700s and how it compares to life today.

Stratford Hall Plantation: Colonial Education

www.stratfordhall.org/learn/teacher/education.php

This site tells about the schooling colonial children received. Other links lead to information about games, music, health, and slavery in colonial times.

About the Author

Ann Heinrichs is the author of more than two hundred books for children and young adults. Most of them cover U.S. and world history, geography, culture, and political affairs. Heinrichs was a children's book editor for many years. Then she worked as an advertising copywriter. An avid traveler, she has toured Europe, Asia, Africa, and the Middle East. Born in Fort Smith, Arkansas, she now lives in Chicago, Illinois. She enjoys bicycling and kayaking.